A Potpourri of Thoughts

Anusha Akella

BookLeaf Publishing

India | USA | UK

Presentation by *BookLeaf Publishing*

Web: www.bookleafpub.com

E-mail: info@bookleafpub.com

ISBN: 9789357615679

First edition 2022

To my paternal grandfather, Late Shri A.V.Surya Narayana Rao garu,

I remain forever indebted to you for inculcating the love of reading & writing in me.

ACKNOWLEDGEMENT

I write this with eternal gratitude in my heart .
Firstly to the almighty for this wonderful life that I have been blessed with.

To my parents , Shri A.Bhujanga Sarma and Smt Madhavi Latha , for everything they have done for me and for having always believed in me;

My husband Siddharth, for all the love and encouragement ;

My sister Pratyusha and My brother in law Kaushik for being my pillars of strength ;

My Mother-in-law Smt Padmavathi and my Father-in-law Shri M.V.R.Eswar for being ever so supportive,

And all my extended family and friends , you all inspire me in many more ways than you can possibly imagine.

My deepest gratitude to both my maternal and paternal grandparents for showering me with their love and affection.

Last but definitely not the least , my heartfelt thanks and gratitude to Bookleaf Publishing, for helping my dream of being published, come true.

Paradise.

Intro: Anguish of a junior doctor as an 85 year old COVID patient approached end of life , without his family by the bedside to bid him goodbye.

"I am sorry.."
"We can't, I am afraid"
"I understand.."
"But the infection.."
"The virus.."
"It is an extremely difficult situation"
"Yes he is comfortable"
"No , he doesn't seem to be in pain"
"Yes we will keep you updated"
"I am sorry but there is an emergency.."
"I have to go.."

My fatigued mind replayed the conversation
Of those I had very many
As I rested my back
After a 12 hour shift
The gentleman's kind face
Flashed in my mind
And his wife's sobs

Rang in my ears

Their 60 years of togetherness
Had come to an end
And the wife was denied
The opportunity to bid farewell

I woke up with a jolt
To the blaring noise
Of Intensive Care Monitors
My eyes frantically scoured
The darkness
For the source of my angst
That was nowhere to be found outside.

I rolled back into a slumber
Hoping this one would last longer

"I am sorry—
You couldn't
Say your goodbyes"

"It's not your fault dear"
He said with an air of tranquillity
He was at peace
Radiating a glow of contentment
Whilst discreetly wiping a tear
Trying to smile

We were going to celebrate
60 years of our wedding
Next week
By the sea

I loved having her arm around mine
Her head on my shoulder
As we strolled along the coast
The waves crashing
Touching our feet
Whisking away the earth underneath

Oh, how she was enchanted
Transported into a world of
Pure, innocent joy
A childish glee
Playing on her face
Whilst she witnessed
The sun going down on the horizon

She despised talks of death
But said, when times comes
We would go together
For she disliked
Walking into sunsets
On her own

Hot tears
Transiently blurring my vision

Streamed down my face
As I looked around

Faint hues of luminous golden yellow
A crisp orange
Played peekaboo
Amongst the bluish white clouds
The sky in all its glory
Looked imperturbable
Unlike my tumultuous self

Filled with anguish
I asked him
If he was upset
About not having the chance
To bid adieu to his beloved

Don't fret, child
He smiled

Life's one and only promise
Is unpredictability
And at times
Life goes out of its way
To honour the word.
I do lament
That my death has been taken away
From me
From my dear ones

But I am also grateful
For having experienced
Life's wonderful adventures
For about 6 decades
With the woman I adore
For how many get to spend
This great amount of their
Time on earth
Amidst such endearment

Do I moan about
Another missed milestone
Whilst the young man in the adjacent bed
Did not live to see his son?

But, I said
Grief cannot be compared
Yours is equally real
And valid
As theirs, isn't it?

Probably, yes
He said,
Sorrow indeed
Cannot be calibrated
Or gauged

We cannot deny our affliction

Yet we can
Gain a perspective
After all
Isn't that what life is all about?
Getting the right viewpoint?
Then why can't
Death be the same as well?

At the end of the day
Isn't death, but a part of life?

The Overthinker

Intro: A glimpse into the mind of an overthinker.

Fear creeps in
As the daylight fades
Twilight comes along
Bringing with it the blades.

The back rests and the battle begins
The same teams, the same fight
As the insomniac in you fidgets
You know its only keeping you up with fright.

Toss and turn around in bed
Was it the body shaming at work?
Was it the 3 year old break up at the back of
your head?
Was it the coldness in your flatmate's smirk?
You know the teams are stronger tonight.

Those love handles seem to love you too much
Those dark circles ain't gonna get any better
Those sickening stares across the street make
you feel so stuck

All those "haters gonna hate" don't get you any
closer.

A sudden clank in the hallway pulls you out of
your covers
"Anabelle?" "Bathsheeba?" You wonder which
one is at your door
And then you find yourself laughing
Could they be any worse than those in your own
head?

You ponder and ponder
And you think of the morrow
I am gonna slip into slumber
Ain't got no time for sorrow

You know life has been kind to you
And you know you ain't returning the favour
Why doesn't the insomniac ever get tired
Why do the same tedious battles don't let you
sleep for few
Why doesn't the night ever get old

You think!
And that's another hour's sleep in the drain!

Curb it here and curb it now
The "over thinker" ain't gonna show you any
love.

Take a Moment.

Intro: A poem on the importance of appreciating your worth.

Hey, it's me
That still, small voice at the back of your head
That you hardly ever listen to
But here I am
A bit louder than usual
Hoping you will
This time.

Let's take a moment
Sit down
Breathe
And commemorate all that you have achieved.

It has been a long day
A long week
A long year
How are you?
Are you okay?

I was there
When you were burning the midnight oil

When you shed tears of frustration, fatigue and
exhaustion
When you did not take the easy route
When you let go of that extra hour of sleep, to
arrive early at work on a weekend
When you couldn't say "NO" to others
When you wouldn't say "YES" to yourself

I was there
When you toiled hard at something you "love"
Yet felt a gaping void in your soul
When you ate all your meals
Hardly even noticing what they were
When you cursed yourself
For eating that chocolate cookie at 3 am
When you repeatedly mentioned to your family
that you want to "quit"
But never did so, cause you are not a "quitter"

I was there
When your eyes grew wide
Expecting that promotion at work
When your palms grew sweaty
As you awaited your boss's feedback
When your heart thumped 10 times faster
At a family gathering,
Looking for an appreciative nod from a
"successful" relative.

Why though?

What is this
Insatiable need for external validation?
Where is the end to this?
Is there an end to this?
Is this the only way you gauge your worth?
Is the entirety of your existence dependent on
someone's approval?
On someone's opinion?
On someone's ability to notice your value?

But, hey
Opinions change, don't they?

Are you telling me that opinions are set in stone?

Are you telling me that your own opinion of
someone has never changed?

You know this is not true.

Then Why
Won't you take a moment
To pat yourself on the back
To congratulate yourself on how far you have
come
To liberate yourself from the clutches of this
imaginary perfection

To take a deep breath and say, "well done, me!"

Why
Do you want to impress someone
Who the society says is "successful"

And what is "success" really?
Isn't success something very subjective?
Something very abstract?
Something which had a very different meaning,
say 20 years ago?

Is it the abundance of materialistic possessions?
Is it having a string of educational degrees
following your name?
Is it being able to run a marathon every year?
Is it pouring your heart out on a canvas?
Is it owning a myriad of branded merchandise?
Is it being able to go on vacations every year?
Is it being contended with yourself?
Is it being able to derive happiness from what
you do?
Is it being able to love deeply and
unconditionally?

You know it could be any
Or all of the above.

Yet you allow yourself

Your worth and your value
To be judged by someone
Who has a very different idea of success

And what's worse
You try to fit into their picture
At the cost of leaving yours,
Empty and Unfulfilled.

So my friend
Celebrate yourself,
Don't wait for an "X" event
Or an "X" person to celebrate you

The very fact that you have come so far
Battling the winds
Fighting the storms
Deserves an applause

Appreciate your worth
Your value
Your existence
And do remember,
Approval comes from within.

Inside the buried memory.

Intro: The poem is about a person suffering from dementia.
The protagonist refers to dementia as 'Bee'.

I see them walking towards me
Mumbling in a language I barely recognize
I hear them mention my name repeatedly
Alas, that's probably all I could analyze.

I hear the incessant buzzing in my head
It has now become a ritual
The Bee, I realise is going no where
The habitat is however, no longer what it was.

Everyday, a young man comes by
Gives me a hug, an endearing smile
But soon turns sad
He is here all day,
His demeanour emanating warmth
His eyes echoing his heartache
And he calls me "Dad".

My bed is clean

Thanks to the lady
She is kind and brings me food
An image of my mother flashes in my eyes
And before I reminisce
The buzzing intensifies

At times I wake up
With a start
It is dark all around,
I shout, I cry, I struggle
Then I see a bunch of familiar
Radiant faces
I fail to place them,
I fail to recollect
Memory is a thing of the past

I get tired when I walk too much
I wonder if the bee ever will
If only I could reciprocate the affection
Of that young man
If only I could see my mother's image
A little longer
If only I could remember those merry people
If only the Bee would leave me in peace.

The Farewell.

Intro: I wrote this poem in the memory of my very dear paternal grandmother.

Walking into the hallway
Clutching my heavy heart
I tried not to fumble
On her memory filled past

Gathering little courage
I took one step at a time
Just like how she taught me
Just like how she did at last

I climbed those stairs where she once sat
Nostalgia hitting me very hard
My soul dangling between what was and what is
My heart choking on those mid-day laughter we
once shared

As I managed to pull myself into the lounge
I was welcomed with a deafening silence
A place that was always filled with her cheer
Could only offer some condolence

I drank up the scene around me
Barely moving an inch
As her swing stared back at me
Empty and blanched

I finally stepped into her room
It was her abode of serenity
The bed and the cot
Which she had once slept on
Were all that remained

I saw her clothes on the shelf
Neatly folded just how she liked
Not knowing they wont be ruffled
Not knowing they wont be worn

I stood there frozen
Her words and actions echoing my thoughts
When I felt a strange warmth
On that cold stone

"Be happy"she had said
"That's what makes me happy"she had said.

I tried to swallow the grief
As I walked out of her room
I tried to smile through my tears
Hoping that she is in peace
Hoping that she is in bliss.

Sandcastle

Intro: A poem about the importance of living in
the present.

A foot in the yester
Brood, ponder and dwell
On matters of little
Significance
On matters of little
Consequence
On a colleague's baseless
Judgement
On a neighbour's
Envious pun

A foot on the morrow
Trepidation, apprehension and angst
The outcome
Of a test
Of a meeting
Of a tete-a-tete with a potential partner

An overlooked "current"
Embedded in the streams
Of perturbation

Over affairs on which
I have but little control
Lost
Now and Forever

The present is all I have
It is my only moment
My glowing, golden beach sand
All set to become a castle
In a fashion
Of my will and desire

And I
Let it slip
Through my fingers
Let it get swallowed
Let it fall prey
To the waves of the bygone
To the torrents of the upcoming

And all I am left
With
The conscience of
A missed opportunity.

Not so Rational.

Intro: A funny story-time poem on my experience of getting a nose piercing.

"Are you ready for this?"
The lady with the longest eye lashes
I've ever seen
Asked with a good natured smile
Holding a piercing gun
To my right nostril.

I squeezed my eyes shut
Trying to tap out the random
Weekday morning shoppers
Staring at me through the glass door
As I tried and failed dismally
To conceal my anxiety
With a ridiculous smile.

"Erm.. remind me, why are we doing this?"
My rational brain chirped
"Cause I've always wanted to!"
Needless to say, this response was by my
not-so-rational
Side of the brain.

"But we've never been so impulsive, we know
nothing about this,
We haven't even watched a single youtube video
about this process"
My rational brain kicked off
"It's okay to be spontaneous at times—-
I overthink all the time and never
Actually end up doing it"
"Are we not too old for this"
My rational brain brought out the big guns
"Infact that was the first question the lady asked
us- how old are you, she said, albeit kindly"
"Look, have you heard of 'you only live once?'
I gotto be a daredevil at times!"
"Huh? Gotto? Really?"
My rational brain was at the fag end of its
patience
"This sounds like some kind of quarter-mid life
crisis at 29!"
"And what's with that god awful ludicrous smile
??"
My rational brain's voice died out with that.

"Are you ready for this"
The kind lady asked me again
This time around
Betraying a hint of impatience

"Okay" I squeaked

As the rational and not-so-rational
Parts of my brain
Entered into a second round of battle
This time about why a nose piercing
Is a bad idea
On a "tomato" shaped nose.

I sat there , quiet as a cat
Expecting a —-
What was I expecting?
A 'Kaboom'
A 'sharp sting'
A scratch?
Some blood?
I imagined myself
Jumping out of the chair
Running on the high street
With my nose swelling by an inch
With Every passing second
An irrational smile of triumph
Plastered on my face

I shuddered
Am I that dramatic?
"Well if we are this impetuous…"
My rational brain was now raising its head again

"All done" the lady beamed
Dragging me out of my reverie

She did look more relieved
Than I was.

She handed me a mirror
As I sighed a breath of relief
Glad that my nose
Had not upgraded
To a pumpkin
From a tomato

I also felt a tiny bit sorry
For the little white titanium stud
That struggled hard to stay afloat
And from getting sucked
Into
My enormous nasal cartilage

Despite the theatricals
I realised that as I walked out
Of the store
I still managed to retain
That frivolous smile of victory
Over my rational brain
On my 29 year old face.

Regrets (Haiku)

Regrets are heavy
So are new beginnings
You choose the weight, Jane.

Power

Intro: This poem starts off with a reference to Game of Thrones and Daenerys Targaryen. For those who haven't watched the series- in the simplest of terms- Daenerys is a character who has been portrayed as someone who is highly passionate about winning her kingdom back and at the same time is very just . In the last two seasons, her character begins to take a U turn and she eventually ends up taking a path very similar to her tyrrant ancestors.

My mind struggled to comprehend
What my eyes
Had virtually witnessed.
My internal screaming wouldn't stop
As I tried hard to make peace
With the collapsing character arc
Both literally and figuratively
Of world-renowned television series

An ardent fan
Of the 8 year long
Fantasy Drama
I was disappointed, to say the least

By Game of Thrones Finale.

A Khaleesi
Who liberated thousands
From the shackles
Of Slavery
Was now burning
Civilians alive

Dumbfounded
I pondered
Desperately trying
To conjure
A cause and effect theory

Is it "Power"
That brings about this devastating change
Or is it
The "Hunger for Power?"

Are tyrants
Indeed ruthless?
Or are they merely cowards?
Afraid of
Losing their ability to exert power and control?

And what is "power" really?
Why is it so addictive?

.. I questioned
As I continued to run
Through the mazes of my mind ..

Where does Power lie?

In a position?
A single person?
A person in that position?
Or the millions
That place their trust
In this one single person?

Perhaps it is neither?
Like Tolstoy said-
Perhaps it is the "relation
Of the men who command
To those they command"

Power feeds on those
Who fail to notice
Or worse
Choose to ignore
The fine line
Between
Fighting to win
And

Fighting to Kill.

Short-lived.

As impermanent
As a fleeting moment
As impermanent
As a night -blooming cereus
As impermanent
As the life span of a caterpillar
Is my time here on earth.

Let me be that joyous moment
The flower that blooms to the fullest
And emerge, a butterfly
In the wake.

What if?

Intro: A different perspective on the very famous
Cinderella and by extension Fairy Tales in
general.

The bluish skies
Enchanted with purple hues
The magical, dreamy
Extravaganza of
Fairy tales
Tug at my heartstrings
For all good reasons
My source of solace
My reassurance of a happy ending
In this uncertain world.

Funny though,
How most of the
Happily, ever afters
Consists of a "Handsome, gallant prince"
Galloping towards
A damsel in distress
To fish them out of
Their misery.

As I ponder,

I worry
At the cognizable impact
These beautiful
Yet stereotyped stories
Have on young minds

Is life's only chance
Of refuge
Dependent on
A someone coming to our rescue?
Can't we be our own
Versions of Gallantry?

What if
In the place of a Prince
Cinderella
Found her own voice?

What if
Cinderella's
Fairy Godmother
Gave her not
A glittery gown and glassy shoes
But helped her find
Her inner strength and Courage
To stand her ground?

What if
Cinderella realised

That her happiness
Was not in an external
Person / Possession
But in herself
Hiding beneath
Monumental load of
Insecurities, self-doubt
And
Poor self-esteem?

But then
Am I getting carried away?
Am I being over analytical?
Over thinking a princess story?
It is a fairy tale after all
Do I just accept it?
The way we accept
The absurdity
Of Glass shoes?

Seasons.

Hues of bright orange
Blind my view
The scattered leaves
Of Fall
Lie Withered, barely alive
Yet full of colour
And beauty
Even in their passing.

The nature's celebration
Of a life well lived
The nature's mockery
Of an inevitable death

The wake is indeed numbing
As the frost takes over
A final goodbye
Au revoir
A farewell,
The final prayers offered
With sleet , snow and ice
Before life "springs " back
With
Vigour and Vitality.

Hope (Haiku)

Hope is but, a ray
Of sunshine, a bleak moment
Filled and lost, forever.

Utopia

The tender warmth
Of the early sunshine
Softening the form
Of the frost
High up in the north

The element transcends
Making its way south
As it blends
Into the ebb and flow
Of the thawing river

Little ripples of exuberance
Appear
As the stream dances
In mirth and joy
Greeting the visitor
With open arms

And off they go
Undulating into eternity
Inseparable
Unflinching of any adversity
Lala land ahead

Moonlight.

Intro: As a huge Harry Potter nerd, there are a few characters who I feel are massively underrated. One of them is Remus Lupin. Apart from being one of the best teachers ever for the trio, Remus is also extremely altruistic. He deserved better. For the uninitiated, Remus is a werewolf. A fate bestowed on him when he was bitten by an evil werewolf as a child.

I tried to write something from his perspective and this is what I came up with.

A source of tranquillity
An icon of romance
A splash of bright white
On a shimmery black canvas
A source of smile

A source of dread
A sign of impending doom
An icon of a painful reminder
Of the monster that I've become

As the great orb illuminates
The lives of commoners

As the world rejoices its comeback
Every fortnight
I, the Lupine
Cower into obscurity
Shudder with fear
Of inflicting this misery
Onto another kid

Glares full of suspicion
Hands itching to cast me out
Witches and Wizards alike
Shrinking away
Retreating from my surroundings
Demonize my existence

For who would trust
"An honest wolf"
Is there a better oxymoron
I hear you snigger

I could lament all I want
The fact remains that
With every full moon
The beast is unleashed
And I am catapulted
From the world that I scarcely belong
To the one that I never will
Survive.

End (Haiku)

As long or short
Life may be, it culminates
In the same cosmos.

The Bride

The spinning wheel came to a halt
The world around her paused
The moment seemed to have frozen in time
And the vows were called.

The innumerable thoughts that kept her
Anxious and fidgety
The inexplainable questions causing the stir
The cliched butterflies
And the atypical fervour
Brought about their might.

It's absolutely normal, don't fret
The world advised
She wasn't afraid, she is not a novice to change
It was a huge step that she was longing to tread
Yet it felt wonderfully unfamiliar to be the one
For her own one

Amidst the chaos of the wedding rituals
She found the unflustered belonging
Which now had to be shared
Between her own kinsfolk and his

A sudden gush of longing to hug her mom
To be her father's little girl
To gossip away with her sister
Overrode their way into her eyes
As they streamed

She walked into the festivities
Embracing the change that has now occurred
With her hand held
Reassurances communicating in silence
As the faith in her decision strengthened.

The Red Camellia.

Intro: A glimpse into an introvert's mind.

The day she dreaded the most had arrived
She entered,
Anxious, distressed and uncomfortable
Her face echoing her emotions
Her eyes desperately searching for a safe spot.

But what is "safe" really? she pondered...

Eventually, she found one
A solitary, basic, dull-looking chair
Positioned away from the centre of the party
Tucked into a corner

She started running towards the lone chair
Racing against ------
Wait, who was she racing against?

Who would want
A desolate, lonesome chair
Amidst an extravagant
Ostentatious crowd
Amidst roars of laughter

Amidst the glory of a celebration

What were they celebrating again?
She could not remember…

All she could think of was "the chair, the chair,
the chair"
As if her life depended on it
And in some ways, it did.

Why was she so keen on this particular chair?
It was by no means fanciful
Or pretty
Or aesthetically pleasing
Yet it was the only thing she could relate to
It promised something----

Some obscurity?
May be
An anonymity?
A certain incognizance?

It was her oasis, in this desert of flamboyance

As she reached the spot and took her seat
A tremendous swooping relief crept over her
form
The insignificance of her position

In this foreign world
Felt liberating.

She looked around in her vicinity
Here she was, away from the glitz and glamour
Of the world
A plain Jane
In a non-existent corner
Of a very real, absolute world.

Her eyes searched for the likes of her
If any
And she saw two others across the great hall
Looking as contended as she did
In their non-fancy chairs

They smiled at her
Warm, acknowledging and understanding
She returned the smile
And realised that they craved the oblivion
As much as she did

At that precise moment
A group of most resplendent looking hosts
Walked towards her
They smiled as they exchanged pleasantries

This smile however
Although polite, lacked something

It wasn't warm
It wasn't unkind
Instead, there was another emotion

"Oh, what is this sentiment", she racked her
brains

"That's it", she thought
"Pity".

She saw that they were sorry for her
The Social Misfit
The simple little Common Daisy in a field of
exotic Orchids.

But was she a Common Daisy?

If only they were a legilimens
Could they look into the mind
Of this maverick
Of the enchanted world she could conjure
Of the dreams that filled her soul to the brim
Of the vivid and vibrant canvases that lay
underneath
That lay camouflaged under her
Sombre exterior

Of the organized chaos of an introverted mind.

Was she a Common Daisy?
Or was she indeed a Red Camellia?

Pitter-Patter

A roar of thunder
Reverberated through the
Shuddering sky
As I walked into my backyard.

The clouds grew darker
The breeze, cooler
And the stage
Has been set
For the first rainfall
Of the season.

Not someone who
Romanticizes the monsoon
I swiftly grabbed my things
In the garden
And headed indoors
Just as the rumbling of the showers
Made its way through

As I attempted to shut the door
The pitter patter
Unleashed a time turner from within
And I stood there, frozen
Transported to much simpler times

Of paper boats
And scraped knees

The little mud puddles that formed
On the streets
Served as "The Thames"
For our paper boat regattas

The joy of hearing "makkha-bhutta"*
The corn vendor announcing his presence
His loud yet friendly voice
Had us running down the road

As we walk back home
Relishing our hot treat
Our school uniforms
Wet, stained, and dishevelled
A car races through
The muddy water puddle
A great splash!

We scream in mock-anger
A second later
We laugh looking at each other
What a mess we were!
And what trouble awaits at home!

The soaking wet feet
Were not a source of inconvenience

The mud splashing driver
Was not a cause of annoyance
The long walk home
In dripping wet uniform
Was not frustrating

The "who won" and "who lost"
Of our
Paper boat Olympics
Was but a moment of pure fun

The "Oh, mum is going to be so angry!!"
Was in fact the fear
That united us all

"Ping"
"Ping"
"Ping"
Notifications from
Multiple social media applications
Wake me up from my reverie
As I shut the door
To my Wi-Fi-free past
And enter
Into my
Heavily filtered
Present.

Ray of Hope.

There once lived a swan
 Her world a hullaballoo
 Beauty camouflaged in flaws
 Her spirit the strongest hue

She battled on
 With the current upstream
 Struggling to catch up
 Hesitant to break a beam

Landing herself in an unfamiliar dawn
She began to swallow the verity
Strong yet vulnerable
She bore a heart of mayhem
Masked under serenity

On one of those days of flounder
A cob flew down,
His wings fluttering
He dabbled along her side

Helping her reach her food with a swing

As he swam past her wake
Sweeping the ruffling ripples with ease
The still waters transpiring her reflection

He made her discover her strength
That was hiding miles beneath

The swan, realising the gesture
Shared the lead
They built their world of dreams
Of desires and aspirations
And on days when the cob
Hit the lows
The swan held up for them both
She was the pillar
For the cob to fall back on

As the moons shined on

The cob and the swan
Made for the strongest team

The obstacles never ceased for either,
But they would now not dither
Their indestructible bond
Holding them together
Valiant and upright.